# Honey-dew and Paradise

Samuel Taylor Coleridge at the birthplace
of English Romantic poetry

*Including a souvenir guide to
Coleridge Cottage*

Weave a circle round him thrice,
And close your eyes with holy dread:
For he on honey-dew hath fed
And drunk the milk of Paradise.

KUBLA KHAN

## Terence and Eliza Sackett

*His thought did not seem to come with labour, and effort;*
*but as if borne on the gusts of genius.*

WILLIAM HAZLITT

On the last day of 1796 Samuel Taylor Coleridge with his wife and baby son moved into Gilbards, a tiny cottage in Nether Stowey on the edge of the Quantock Hills in Somerset. Three years of poetic creativity were about to begin.

'The lovely shapes and sounds intelligible/Of that eternal language'. The words come from *Frost at Midnight*, which Coleridge wrote in his Nether Stowey cottage in 1798. The shapes and sounds were those of the landscape, the 'sea, hill and wood' which he describes in the poem, that natural world to which he responded so intensely during his time in Somerset. Coleridge, with Wordsworth, who was living nearby, succeeded in creating a new language, a new way of writing, 'the real language of men in a state of vivid sensation', as Wordsworth put it, which helped to break the mould of the formal classicism of the 18th century. The poems that Coleridge wrote helped give birth to the Romantic movement, and changed for ever the way we look at the world – and at poetry.

It was while he was living in Nether Stowey that Coleridge wrote the poems that he is remembered best for today: *Kubla Khan, The Rime of the Ancient Mariner, Christabel, Frost at Midnight, This Lime Tree Bower my Prison*. Here he collaborated with Wordsworth to produce *Lyrical Ballads*, perhaps the most momentous partnership in English poetry.

Coleridge's life was not an easy one. Burdened with an addiction to opium, and with a wayward personality, he suffered from feelings of isolation and despair. Yet he was amazingly productive. As well as writing poetry, he was an illuminating literary critic, lecturer, philosopher, journalist, political activist, and a dazzling talker. He had a voracious appetite for knowledge, and wrote to his friend and publisher Joseph Cottle: 'I would thoroughly know Mechanics, Hydrostatics, Optics, and Astronomy, Botany, Metallurgy, Fossilism, Chemistry, Geology, Anatomy, Medicine – then the *mind of man* – then the *minds of men* – in all Travels, Voyages and Histories.'

To the end of his life his poetry bears witness to his spontaneous delight in nature. 'Never saw I his likeness', wrote his friend Charles Lamb, 'nor probably the world can see again'.

# A TOUR OF THE COTTAGE

## The floor plan in 1797

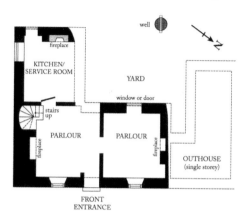

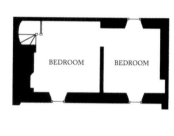

## The floor plan today

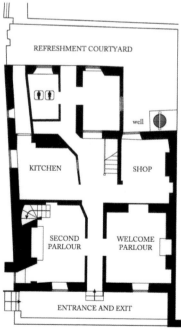

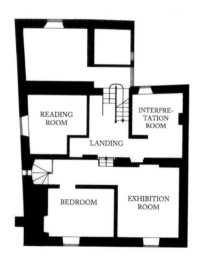

# 1 THE WELCOME PARLOUR

Welcome to Coleridge Cottage. It is a small house, and in Coleridge's time it was even smaller. When Coleridge arrived it was draughty and dirty, and it was overrun with mice. Yet within what was little better than a hovel Coleridge wrote the greatest poetry of his life, the poems for which we remember him best today – *The Rime of the Ancient Mariner*, *Christabel*, *Frost at Midnight*, and *This Lime Tree Bower My Prison*. It is as if this small, humble space concentrated and refined his immense intellect and his soaring imagination to distil a new kind of poetry.

CAROLINE TAYLOR

This parlour is where Coleridge entertained his friends. Young, passionate, and radical in their views, they included his oldest friend the writer Charles Lamb; Coleridge's Stowey patron Tom Poole; the publisher Joseph Cottle; John Thelwall, widely regarded as a dangerous revolutionary; Tom Wedgwood the potter; and above all the poet William Wordsworth and his sister Dorothy, at that time living nearby at Alfoxton House (spelt *Alfoxden* by the Wordsworths). They would talk long into the night, their conversation eager and even heated. Coleridge and Wordsworth would discuss poetry; it was from this corner of Somerset that their revolutionary *Lyrical Ballads* anthology – and in large measure the Romantic Movement – was born.

NT IMAGES / ANDREAS VON EINSIEDEL

No descriptions or pictures exist of the cottage interiors in Coleridge's time, and only a few objects here belonged to or relate directly to Coleridge. Instead, the rooms have been arranged with furniture and objects of the period, but they are not unique or precious. Visitors are welcome to pick things up for a closer look, rummage in the drawers, sit on the chairs, and imagine themselves as Coleridge's guests.

Some of the objects in this parlour suggest the day of the Coleridges' arrival in Stowey: there are boxes and crates to unpack, and piles of books to arrange in the bookcase. A time of intense creativity is about to begin.

# 2 SARA'S KITCHEN

Sara Coleridge was a well-brought-up, well-educated young woman, used to the genteel social life of Bristol. It must have been hard for her to adjust to life in a small, primitive country cottage, and above all to the gruelling work involved in running the household from this very basic kitchen.

NT IMAGES / ANDREAS VON EINSIEDEL

When Sara was living here this room was probably smaller and darker than it is now – not at all convenient for carrying out the hard, dirty tasks she had to do. The water needed for cooking, cleaning the house and washing the clothes had to be drawn from the well in the yard and heated over the open fire. There was no range or oven. This meant that Sara could have cooked stews, pottage and boiled puddings over the fire, but pies and meat for roasting had to be taken to the baker's to be cooked there.

The kitchen table and dresser, and the crocks and pots, are typical examples of the kinds of kitchen furniture and equipment that Sara would have used. Notice the candles hanging on the side of the dresser, and the candle box on the wall: these are tallow candles, made from animal fat, and they needed to be kept high off the floor so that mice and rats could not eat them. The Coleridges would also have used rush lights – you can find some in the table drawer. These were made by peeling rushes and dipping the pith in animal fat, and they were held in a rush nib.

Look at the floor tiles, which were revealed during the recent restoration of the cottage. They had been hidden beneath a thin skim of concrete, protected by layers of newspaper dating from the early 1900s – you can see the traces of 20th-century ink on the much older tiles. The tiles were probably added after Coleridge's time when the cottage was an inn.

NT IMAGES / ANDREAS VON EINSIEDEL

# 3 THE SECOND PARLOUR

This was one of the two living rooms lying left and right of the front door which was used by Coleridge and his family.

The big fireplace that dominates the room is probably the one beside which Coleridge was sitting when he wrote *Frost at Midnight*, describing in its opening lines how 'at my side / My cradled infant slumbers peacefully'. The

*The Second Parlour and the door to the passage*

cradle displayed here today is a modern replica of cradles depicted in 18th-century paintings; cradles were often made of willow, like this one, as they could be hosed down to clean them!

The fireplace was revealed during the recent restoration of the cottage; it used to be hidden behind an early 19th-century fireplace like the one in the Welcome Parlour. In his letters Coleridge told how smoke used to billow into the room. After the fireplace had been restored by the National Trust the chimney still smoked. However, that problem has now finally been solved.

*The restored fireplace and replica cradle*

The family may have eaten their meals in this room, and Sara could rest the pots and pans on the trivet beside the fire to keep the food warm. Light meals, like Coleridge's favourite toasted cheese, could be cooked here. Sara would toast the bread on the toasting fork, then heat the salamander and pass it over the cheese to brown it.

# 4 THE BEDROOM

The bedroom is furnished simply, even sparsely, for the Coleridges had no money to spare for luxuries, and there is not enough space in this little cottage for grand furnishings.

The room is presented to suggest the events that strained the relationship between Coleridge and Sara. Looking after small children – Hartley and Berkeley, the baby – kept Sara busy. Notice the pot of yellow sulphur, or brimstone. When Hartley was three he caught scabies, and the cure was to paint him all over with brimstone. Sara was 'tired off her legs' fumigating the house. Coleridge was no help – he retreated to a corner 'undisturbed as a Toad in a Rock' – but Hartley enjoyed the fuss, singing 'I be a funny fellow, and my name is Brimstonello'!

Another problem for Sara was the Wordsworths. Constrained by domestic tasks, Sara could not take part in the talks and long walks with them that Coleridge enjoyed, and she found it hard to get on with Dorothy Wordsworth. Sara's clothes at the foot of the bed have been left there by Dorothy – she used to borrow Sara's dresses to go walking with Coleridge and William and, not content with despising the clothes for being out of date, she once even returned a dress muddy at the hem.

Tragedy came in 1799. Coleridge was studying in Germany – he was away for a year – when Berkeley fell ill. For weeks Sara was up all night nursing him; we can see that the bedclothes are disarranged, and the candles are burned right down. His lungs were affected, he had a high fever, and he could hardly breathe. The baby died in Sara's arms in Bristol. When Coleridge eventually heard of Berkeley's death, he did not hurry home. Sara felt abandoned, and Coleridge could not come to terms with his guilty feelings. It was the beginning of the end of their relationship, and of their happy time in Stowey.

7

# 5 THE EXHIBITION ROOM

When Coleridge lived here, sources suggest there were three bedrooms crammed into the small space upstairs. The Coleridges' lodger, a young man called Charles Lloyd, stayed here briefly in 1797 – he suffered from violent epileptic fits, and Coleridge frequently had to stay up all night attempting to soothe him.

*Coleridge's inkstand*

Coleridge's friends slept here too when they visited. One of them was John Thelwall, the radical, who had earlier been tried for treason; he was regarded as one of the most dangerous men in Britain – at this time a French invasion was feared, and Thelwall was believed to have Revolutionary sympathies.

Another visitor was Charles Lamb, the writer, and another was Wordsworth himself, just before he and his sister Dorothy came to live at nearby Alfoxton.

Today this room contains Coleridge memorabilia, personal objects and portraits that enable us to feel closer to him. They include pictures and letters referring to Coleridge's early life in Ottery St Mary, and a sword reputed to be his. This reminds us of Coleridge's attempt to escape debt and gain his family's approval by enlisting as a soldier in 1793. Eventually his family managed to secure his discharge from the army – on the grounds that he was insane!

*The Historic Corridor from the Exhibition Room with the Bedroom on the left*

Other items include letters and manuscripts, early editions of his poetry, a poem by his friend Thomas Poole, and even several locks of Coleridge's hair. His grand, elaborate inkstand, seemingly incongruous in this little cottage, reminds us of the fame and relative wealth that was to come.

*A lock of Coleridge's hair*

# 6 THE INTERPRETATION ROOM
# 7 THE READING ROOM

The Interpretation Room and the Reading Room are in the Victorian extension to the old cottage. In the late 19th century the cottage became an inn, and was much altered and enlarged. In 1893 a committee of admirers of Coleridge began to raise funds to preserve the cottage, and put up the memorial tablet on its front wall. In 1908 they were able to buy the cottage, and in 1909 it was transferred to the National Trust. Professor William Knight, editor of Wordsworth's poems and an energetic member of the committee, wrote:

*'It is my belief that these 'outward and visible signs' of the life that was led by our greatest poets, in the places where they wrote their immortal works, are valuable national assets: and that they will be welcomed by posterity as amongst its most precious heirlooms.'*

*A bust of Coleridge,
by Sir Hamo Thornycroft*

TERENCE SACKETT

*Maquette of the
Ancient Mariner
statue at Watchet*

**The Interpretation Room**

Here you can find out more about Coleridge's poetry and the birth of the Romantic movement, and discover how his writing has inspired poets, artists and musicians ever since.

On the table are paper, ink and quill pens. You can write a poem of your own, and see it displayed on the wall. Have a look at the view from the window; the glass is 'etched' with a picture of what the view was like in the past.

**The Reading Room**

Here you can relax and get to know Coleridge better. His bust, by Sir Hamo Thornycroft, will keep you company as you sit on the sofa and listen to his poetry through the headphones. You can browse through the books in the bookcase and read in peace here for as long as you like.

A portrait of Tom Poole, Coleridge's Stowey friend and patron, hangs on the wall, and in the corner is a maquette of the sculpture of the Ancient Mariner by Alan B Herriot. If you visit Watchet, you can see the sculpture itself standing beside the harbour from which Coleridge imagined the Mariner sailing.

# 8 THE GARDEN

Coleridge greatly valued his garden and orchard, and would show them with pride to visiting friends. The garden which survives today was chiefly an apple orchard when Coleridge lived here and was twice as wide as it is now. Here he would sit with Sara on the 'tree crooked earth-ward' and would hold Hartley in his arms looking up at the stars.

When the Coleridges first arrived, the plan was to be as self-sufficient as possible. Coleridge was determined to grow his own vegetables, and he kept two pigs, three geese and three ducks. However, reading, writing, seeing his friends and walking on the Quantocks proved more attractive pursuits, and the garden soon contained more weeds than anything else.

At the far end of his garden Coleridge had direct access into Tom Poole's garden, a detached area, now built over, that stood behind Tom Poole's house and tan pits. It was there, in Tom Poole's jasmine-covered arbour, shaded by a lime tree, that Coleridge wrote *This Lime Tree Bower My Prison*. Sara had spilt a skillet of boiled milk and scalded his foot, just at a time when Charles Lamb had come to Stowey – he was unable to walk with his dearest friend on the Quantocks. Sitting in the bower, sad to be alone, he was soothed by the sights and sounds of the garden, and felt it good to 'contemplate/With lively joy the joys we cannot share'.

Today a new bower has been created, made from material coppiced in the Quantock woods, a lovely place to sit and enjoy the wild flowers. Nearer the house is a more formal cottage garden, planted with the flowers and shrubs typical of Coleridge's time.

In the yard behind the Cottage is the old well, from which the Coleridges had to draw their water. It has been re-lined with brick, probably in the Victorian era. It is a dizzying experience to gaze into the depths – it is about 14m deep, and the water level varies according to the rainfall (see photograph on page 31).

# *imagine* ...
## the Coleridges arrive at Nether Stowey

*Samuel Taylor Coleridge*
*1772-1834*

> ❝ I mean to work very hard – as cook, butler, scullion, shoe-cleaner, occasional nurse, gardener, hind, pig protector, chaplain, secretary, poet, reviewer … I shall keep no servant, and shall cultivate my land-acre and my wise-acres as well as I can … ❞
>
> S T COLERIDGE TO TOM POOLE, 11 DECEMBER 1796

*31 December 1796.* The last day of the year, and bitterly cold. A wagon rattles and slides its way up Lime Street from Bridgwater through slicks of mud, the furniture lashed precariously on top straining at the ropes.

A dog sidles over, sniffs a wheel, then disappears down a passage. Someone shouts from the poorhouse. No one's watching – icy gusts are discouraging even the most inquisitive village children. And, as any villager could tell you, Stowey families shuffle their belongings from cottage to cottage all the time, chasing cheaper rents.

The wagon pulls up at the far end of the street. A young man jumps down and trips into the gutter, drenching his boots in freezing water. He laughs out loud.

'Here we are, Sara! Gilbards!'

He stands back, hands on hips, and looks up at the tiny cottage with its sodden walls and sagging thatch. The driver's unknotting the ropes – he wants to get on his way, having been subjected to a monologue for the entire journey: a stream of chatter about the young man's wonderful Stowey friend Tom Poole, the manifold joys of fatherhood, the minutiae of working a vegetable patch, and metaphysical ruminations on the German philosopher Immanuel Kant. He was also threatened with an introduction to the greatest poet in England, the mighty William Wordsworth. The young man's eyes flash. 'Let's hurry and unload. I must run over and see Poole! He'll want to know we're here.'

*An impression of Gilbards before its Victorian enlargement, drawn by E H New in 1914*

*A depiction of the Bedroom as it was in Coleridge's time, by E H New, drawn in 1914*

The young woman slumped in the seat beside the driver, teeth chattering, sighs and shifts her baby to the crook of her other elbow. 'Sam, let's get a fire going. I need to feed Hartley.'

Inside, it's poky. She sniffs anxiously at the damp air, then masks the baby's face with a protective hand. She peers into the darkness of the two downstairs rooms, and picks her way through mouse droppings to the tiny back kitchen with its chill tiled floor and simple hearth. No oven.

'Poole didn't exaggerate about it being a hovel, did he?'

But Coleridge isn't listening, he's clattering up and down the narrow stairs. 'Bedrooms, Sara! Three. One for us, one for Nanny, one for our lodger, dear Charles. Well, what do you think? A bargain at eight guineas a year, eh?'

Hartley is wailing in Sara's arms. 'Sam, I'm not sure, it's damp and miserable. And Hartley's cold and hungry, we must get on.'

'Sara, Sara. I'll make it wonderful, I promise. Hartley will love it.' He runs a finger across the baby's cheek and kisses his wife.

He and the driver heave boxes of books and the few bits of furniture – a cupboard, some chairs and a table – off the wagon and carry them through the front door into the main parlour.

'Go and find some kindling, Sam.' But Coleridge is halfway up the garden, leaping the gate and hurrying through the orchard, on his way to Tom Poole's.

*Lime Street in the 1890s, with Gilbards (Coleridge Cottage) on the left, then used as an inn*

# QUANTOCK ADVANCE AND RETREAT

Samuel Taylor Coleridge was just twenty-four when he and his family arrived at Nether Stowey on New Year's Eve, 1796.

For him it was a simultaneous advance and retreat, a paradox that might have fascinated the philosopher Kant whom he so much admired. Coleridge was fleeing the nervous tension caused by agonizing neuralgia, his reputation as a dangerous radical and Jacobin (he had bravely spoken out against slavery in Bristol, which was the centre of the trade in England), and the temptations of the city that kept him from his aspiration to be a great poet. He was also stricken by his failure to earn a satisfactory income

Tom Poole

life at Stowey would bring the period of calm, self-sufficiency and creativity he desperately needed. He would write, pursue his enquiries into German philosophy, and support his family by cultivating his garden. A short walk away were the beautiful Quantock Hills where he would gain inspiration, and where his son Hartley could 'wander like a breeze' in healthy freedom. Of equal importance would be daily contact with his new friend Tom Poole. Poole was a local tanner and farmer; he had little formal education, but was no country bumpkin. He was bright, enquiring, and courageously outspoken. Like Coleridge he was regarded as a radical, and was branded as 'the most dangerous person in the county of Somerset' by government officials. The two men looked forward to a period of sustained mutual support.

*'Upon smooth Quantock's airy ridge we roved …'*
*William Wordsworth, 'The Prelude'*

from writing – his short-lived political and philosophical periodical *The Watchman* had left him with nothing but debts to the printer.

### A fresh start

The scheme for a utopian community in America (Pantisocracy) that he had planned with Robert Southey had come to nothing. He was hoping that a new

### Coleridge settles in

It had been a long and difficult haul finding somewhere to live in Stowey. The possibility of renting a farmhouse at nearby Adscombe had fallen through, leaving Gilbards in Stowey's poorest street as a last resort. Even Poole had been dubious about the Coleridges taking it on. However, the irrepressible Coleridge dismissed Poole's reservations.

Within a short time he was writing enthusiastically to his publisher and friend Joseph Cottle:

*'We arrived safe – our house is set to rights – we are all, Maid, Wife, Bratling, & self, remarkably well. Mrs Coleridge likes Stowey & loves Thomas Poole, & his Mother, who love her – a communication has been made from our orchard into T. Poole's garden ...'*

Another letter to his radical friend John Thelwall, sent just over a month after the move, gave another glowing account of progress:

*'We are very happy, and my little David Hartley grows a sweet boy ... I raise potatoes and all manner of vegetables; have an orchard; and shall raise corn (with the spade) enough for my family.*

*We have two pigs, and ducks and geese ...'*

Inside the cottage, the fires smoked abominably, and Coleridge had plans to 'Rumfordise' them, which involved narrowing the chimney neck to increase the draught. It seems likely that this remained yet another of his unaccomplished plans.

Out in the garden Coleridge was hard at work clearing the ground to grow the all-important vegetables. He planned to make cider from the apples growing in his 'sweet orchard' to refresh his friends. He felt certain they would want to join him in his new-found arcadia. Like so much in the poet's life, he had it all planned. But would it come to fruition?

## 'A poet's eye in a fine frenzy rolling'

| Aged 23 | Aged 24 | Aged 32 | Aged 42 |
| Pieter Vandyke | Robert Hancock | James Northcote | Washington Allston |

'My face unless when animated with immediate eloquence, expresses great Sloth, & great, indeed, almost ideotic good nature. 'Tis a mere carcase of a face: fat, flabby, & expressive chiefly of inexpression ...' COLERIDGE ON HIMSELF, LETTER TO THELWALL 1796

'At first I thought him very plain, that is, for about three minutes: he is pale and thin, has a wide mouth, thick lips, and not very good teeth, longish loose-growing half-curling rough black hair. But if you hear him speak for five minutes you think no more of them. His eye is large and full ... it has more of the "poet's eye in a fine frenzy rolling" than I ever witnessed.' DOROTHY WORDSWORTH

'His forehead was broad and high, light as if built on ivory, with large projecting eyebrows, and his eyes rolling beneath them, like a sea with darkened lustre ...His mouth was gross, voluptuous, open, eloquent; his chin good-humoured and round; but his nose, the rudder of the face, the index of the will, was small, feeble, nothing ...' WILLIAM HAZLITT, 'THE LIBERAL' 1822

# *imagine* ...
## a frosty night, flickering firelight, the birth of a poem

> Hartley fell down and hurt himself – I caught him up crying & screaming – & ran out of doors with him, – The Moon caught his eye – he ceased crying immediately – & his eyes & the tears in them, how they glittered in the Moonlight!

S T COLERIDGE, NOTEBOOKS, *c.* JANUARY 1798

*Laudanum bottles*

*February 1798.* A chill, frosty day. Coleridge, ever prone to illness in winter, had been awake much of the night with neuralgia. Miserable and fidgety, he'd sat all day listlessly poking the fire, nursing his agonised face.

Now it's late afternoon, and the pain's still nagging. He looks down Lime Street from the window of the second parlour. Late afternoon and dusk. Will it still be open? Banging the door shut, he sets off and ducks in through the door of Lewis the apothecary, called by the Over Stowey vicar William Holland 'Little Lewis the monkey'. Coleridge always tries to resist buying laudanum (opium dissolved in alcohol) from Lewis, but today with his face in agony he gives in.

Back at Gilbards, he settles down for the evening by the fire with a book. The laudanum dulls his agony. Sara, ever attentive to her husband's ailments and fretful moods, makes him toasted cheese over the flames.

A happy family time, despite the pain! He's feeling optimistic. The January offer of 'an annuity for life of £150' from the philanthropic Wedgwood brothers, Josiah and Tom, has surprised and delighted him. He's settled his printer's bill, and Sara can walk down Lime Street with her head held high again, knowing that local tradesmen aren't chasing her for money. He's with the Wordsworths most days, and he's writing again, working on his medieval romance *Christabel*, finishing *The Rime of the Ancient Mariner*, and excitedly experimenting

*Hartley, Coleridge's first child*

15

with an innovative new form of conversational poetic language. And Sara is pregnant again.

Finally, Sara yawns, settles Hartley in his wicker cradle, kisses her husband, and climbs the stairs to bed.

Silence. 'The inmates of my cottage, all at rest.' With his son asleep at his side, Coleridge stares into the glowing flames of the fire. He slips into a reverie and imagines a childhood for Hartley very different from his own. Hartley will be a child of Nature, and 'wander like a breeze / By lakes and sandy shores'. In this Quantock paradise 'all seasons shall be sweet' to him. Here they are far from the 'the great city, pent 'mid cloisters dim', where Coleridge had been so miserable as a boy, adrift from his beloved family and his birthplace at Ottery St Mary in Devon.

An owl hoots outside in the frosty night. He goes over to his writing desk, reaches for his notebook, and begins to write. The glowing embers, the frosty street outside, the bright moonlight, his sleeping son – all these elements combine into *Frost at Midnight*, one of his best-loved poems.

*The writing desk in the Second Parlour*

# Frost at Midnight

The Frost performs its secret ministry,
Unhelped by any wind. The owlet's cry
Came loud—and hark, again! loud as before.
The inmates of my cottage, all at rest,
Have left me to that solitude, which suits
Abstruser musings: save that at my side
My cradled infant slumbers peacefully.
'Tis calm indeed! so calm, that it disturbs
And vexes meditation with its strange
And extreme silentness. Sea, hill, and wood,
This populous village! Sea, and hill, and wood,
With all the numberless goings-on of life,
Inaudible as dreams! the thin blue flame
Lies on my low-burnt fire, and quivers not;
Only that film, which fluttered on the grate,
Still flutters there, the sole unquiet thing.
Methinks, its motion in this hush of nature
Gives it dim sympathies with me who live,
Making it a companionable form,
Whose puny flaps and freaks the idling Spirit
By its own moods interprets, every where
Echo or mirror seeking of itself,
And makes a toy of Thought.

                                  But O! how oft,
How oft, at school, with most believing mind,
Presageful, have I gazed upon the bars,
To watch that fluttering stranger ! and as oft
With unclosed lids, already had I dreamt
Of my sweet birth-place, and the old church-tower,
Whose bells, the poor man's only music, rang
From morn to evening, all the hot Fair-day,
So sweetly, that they stirred and haunted me
With a wild pleasure, falling on mine ear
Most like articulate sounds of things to come!
So gazed I, till the soothing things, I dreamt,
Lulled me to sleep, and sleep prolonged my dreams!
And so I brooded all the following morn,
Awed by the stern preceptor's face, mine eye

Fixed with mock study on my swimming book:
Save if the door half opened, and I snatched
A hasty glance, and still my heart leaped up,
For still I hoped to see the stranger's face,
Townsman, or aunt, or sister more beloved,
My play-mate when we both were clothed alike!

Dear Babe, that sleepest cradled by my side,
Whose gentle breathings, heard in this deep calm,
Fill up the interspersèd vacancies
And momentary pauses of the thought!
My babe so beautiful! it thrills my heart
With tender gladness, thus to look at thee,
And think that thou shalt learn far other lore,
And in far other scenes! For I was reared
In the great city, pent 'mid cloisters dim,
And saw nought lovely but the sky and stars.
But thou, my babe! shalt wander like a breeze
By lakes and sandy shores, beneath the crags
Of ancient mountain, and beneath the clouds,
Which image in their bulk both lakes and shores
And mountain crags: so shalt thou see and hear
The lovely shapes and sounds intelligible
Of that eternal language, which thy God
Utters, who from eternity doth teach
Himself in all, and all things in himself.
Great universal Teacher! he shall mould
Thy spirit, and by giving make it ask.

Therefore all seasons shall be sweet to thee,
Whether the summer clothe the general earth
With greenness, or the redbreast sit and sing
Betwixt the tufts of snow on the bare branch
Of mossy apple-tree, while the nigh thatch
Smokes in the sun-thaw; whether the eave-drops fall
Heard only in the trances of the blast,
Or if the secret ministry of frost
Shall hang them up in silent icicles,
Quietly shining to the quiet Moon.

*February 1798*

# *imagine* ...
## a walk with Coleridge
## through Nether Stowey

*Charles Lamb*

❝ Citizen John, this is a fine place to talk treason in!'
'Nay! Citizen Samuel, it is rather a place to make a
man forget that there is any necessity for treason!' ❞
Coleridge to John Thelwall, the Quantocks, 1797
FROM S T COLERIDGE 'TABLE TALK' (1830)

*William Wordsworth*

*July 1797.* Voices. Laughter. Clattering. Sara, unable to
sleep. And hour upon hour the excited monologue of her
husband, with just the occasional brief interruption. Some
peace and quiet, Samuel, please.

Visitors at Gilbards: John Thelwall the notorious
Jacobin and revolutionary, the writer Charles Lamb, and
the Wordsworths. And, of course, Tom Poole, though Sara
knows he won't be feeling at his best without sleep and with
a busy tannery to run.

Five o'clock. She sighs and turns over. Please, Samuel, let me have one more
hour's sleep before I do the breakfasts.

At nine Coleridge ushers his party out into the street so that Thelwall can
view his new country idyll. The sky is already dark with heavy rain clouds, and
Coleridge tells Thelwall that by dinner time Lime Street will be 'an impassable
Hog-stye'. Straight away they are forced to the side of the road by coaches being
whipped along the turnpike to Minehead. Stowey villagers nudge each other and

whisper, staring at Thelwall
with distaste. What's he doing
here? Up to no good.

Ah! Coleridge spots a
pretty young girl he met at a
dance at the Rose and Crown.
Forgetting his aching face, he
rushes over, unable to resist
joking and punning with her.
Then the party pick their way
through a rabble of fluttering
chickens, and stop to warm
their hands over the farrier's furnace. Ragged children (Coleridge calls them
Stowey's nightingales) are making a racket at the windows of the poorhouse.

Moving on, they cup their hands to peer through the window of 29 Lime Street,
the clockmaker's shop. 'There's a man after your own heart, Thelwall.' Inside, James

*Lime Street in the late 1800s, Coleridge Cottage on the right*

'Conjuror' Coles, oblivious of the noise and the faces at his window, is cutting fine-toothed clock wheels. Though Coleridge infuriates his friends with his total disregard for time and deadlines, he relishes talking to Stowey's timekeeper, as he, too, is a radical and democrat. His wife Catherine is also a good friend to Sara.

The sole on one of Coleridge's boots is flapping. Should he go into Price the shoemaker's? As an inveterate walker, Coleridge was a regular customer. Five years later he was to walk across Scotland with the Wordsworths, covering a prodigious 263 miles in just eight days. Part of the time he went barefoot, having forgotten to take his walking boots. Now he thinks of poor Sara, struggling to balance the household budget. What's a wet foot when compared with Hartley's welfare?

At its eastern end, Lime Street meets St Mary Street and Castle Street, and they stop at the timber-framed market cross, with its turret, clock and bell. It's the Tuesday market, and the cross is thronged with Quantock farmers' wives selling produce from baskets.

Milton, the Stowey carrier, has stopped to water his horse at the trough, ready to depart for Bridgwater, his cart loaded down with packages and boxes. Coleridge runs across to him. 'No, Mr Coleridge, I can't wait. I'm late already. Your parcel'll have to go Thursday. I don't care if it is for one of your grand friends.'

*Stowey's market cross in 1796*

The cart rattles off, with the poet left standing in the street gazing after it. 'So, Mr Catcott and the Bristol library must wait for their overdue books. And I must pay a 5s fine. How they expect me to wade through 2,000 pages of Greek in three weeks is beyond me.'

# THE STOWEY COLERIDGE KNEW

Stowey's street plan is medieval in origin. Though the street structure looks deceptively simple, out of sight behind the façades and frontages there is a labyrinth of yards and gardens, threaded by paths and alleyways. The gardens – long, narrow strips of land stretching out behind each cottage – were burgage plots, rented out by the Lord of the Manor in medieval times. They were used as kitchen gardens and for grazing livestock, although Tom Poole built his tannery complex over a considerable area of the ground behind Castle Street.

The 1750 map below shows the village that Coleridge would have known. At the top are the glebe fields, from which the parish priest derived an income. These are now covered by the houses of Coleridge Crescent and Mill Lane. Orchards were everywhere – cider making was a significant industry in the

*Castle Street by E H New (1914)*

late 18th century, and the village had its own cider mill in Castle Street.

Today, most two-bedroomed cottages in Stowey are lived in by just two or three people. Those same cottages in Coleridge's time were home to six, eight or ten inhabitants, all fighting for space. Gilbards, too, must have felt cramped, claustrophobic and noisy, offering precious little privacy, and with only chamber pots for sanitation.

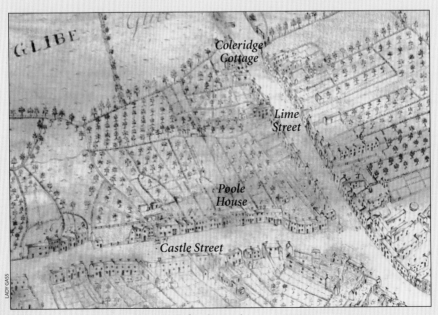

*Nether Stowey in 1750*

## St Mary Street

This was a street of inns, substantial houses, and Stowey Farm. On the left was the Rose and Crown which held dances and social events. Across the road was the Globe Inn. Coleridge would have been shocked if he had known that just a month after Thelwall's visit the Globe would have a visitor who would bring about the end of the Quantock idyll.

Further along the street was the toll house for the Bridgwater Turnpike and the Old House that Tom Poole moved into from Castle Street in 1802.

## Castle Street

Castle Street presents a scene of great charm today with its old stone cottages and cobbled pavements. However, in Coleridge's time people had none of the fond feelings about old buildings that we have. Given the opportunity, it's likely that most of the cottagers would have happily swapped their cramped houses for new bungalows if they had existed – not least Sara Coleridge.

The stream from the Quantocks that tumbles down the side of the street – Coleridge's 'Dear Gutter' – would not have been so crystal clear. Poole regularly opened his tannery sluices into it, releasing stinking residues from what Coleridge called his 'Tartarean pits'.

A little along Castle Street Poole's beautiful and spacious old house had been given a fashionable Georgian frontage. Further up is Castle Hill House, another old building refreshed with a Georgian façade. Here Coleridge's friend John Cruikshank lived – it was Cruikshank who had the dream about the 'spectre-ship' that sparked the idea for *The Rime of the Ancient Mariner*. The house was a haven for Sara, and she would meet here for tea with her friend Anna Cruikshank, who had a baby of Hartley's age.

*Poole House in Castle Street*

22

*Castle Street in the late 1800s, with Poole House on the right with a shop front, now removed*

# Dangerous revolutionaries?

The visit to Stowey by the radical John Thelwall caused serious problems for Coleridge and the Wordsworths. Local people were already suspicious of the trio's wanderings at night over the Quantock Hills. Could they be in the pay of the French? Fears of an invasion were rife, so much so that the Home Office sent down an agent called Walsh to investigate

*John Thelwall*

*The type of hat worn by John Thelwall*

their suspicious activities and wild political talk. He stayed at the Globe Inn (now Clock House in St Mary Street) during August 1797. Though the suspicions proved groundless the damage had been done, and within a year the Wordsworths' tenancy of their Alfoxton house had been terminated. The poet and his sister left for Germany and then moved back to the Lake District for good. Coleridge was soon to follow.

It was ironic that Coleridge was still being cast as a dangerous radical. He had moved to Stowey to escape politics and to live a simple country life. In his poem *Fears in Solitude*, written in April 1798, he expressed his fears: 'What uproar and what strife may now be stirring / This way or that way o'er these silent hills—/ Invasion, and the thunder and the shout, / And all the crash of onset …'

As he sat in a quiet dell overlooking the village he wrote:

> And now, beloved Stowey! I behold
> Thy church-tower, and, methinks, the four huge elms
> Clustering, which mark the mansion of my friend;
> And close behind them, hidden from my view,
> Is my own lowly cottage, where my babe
> And my babe's mother dwell in peace!

This tranquil refuge from the outside world was not to last.

# *imagine* ...
## a walk across the Quantocks to Alfoxden to see the Wordsworths

❛ 'The Giant Wordsworth – God love him! ... he has written near 1200 lines of a blank verse, superior, I hesitate not to aver, to any thing in our language which any way resembles it. ❜ S T COLERIDGE TO JOSEPH COTTLE, MARCH 1798

21 February. Coleridge came in the morning.
22 February. Coleridge came in the morning to dinner.
23 February. William walked with Coleridge in the morning.
FROM DOROTHY WORDSWORTH'S 'ALFOXDEN JOURNAL' (1798)

*May 1798.* Coleridge is climbing the Quantock Hills with the publisher Joseph Cottle. They're on their way to Alfoxden to visit the Wordsworths. Coleridge is keen for Cottle to hear the poems they've written for the proposed anthology *Lyrical Ballads*. Chattering away and rarely pausing for breath, Coleridge weaves from side to side of the path, bounding ahead one moment, then stopping short the next to stare at a hedgerow plant or to scribble in his notebook.

Quantock woods

The two men splash their way through a stream. Its waters will soon be tumbling down Castle Street. They pass a settlement of isolated huts at the edge of Bin Combe woods, and Coleridge stops for a word with the family of broomsquires, who are binding heather and birch twigs to make besoms for Taunton market.

The pair take a sharp turn uphill, forcing a path through trailing brambles, then stop to catch their breath at a gate. Refreshed, they puff their way to the top of the field and meet the Coach Road that winds steeply up from the Minehead turnpike to pass Dead Woman's Ditch on the Quantock ridge.

Smoke rises from charcoal burners' fires in Five Lords below. Cottle is shocked and horrified to hear about the young charcoal burner, John Walford, who was hanged on a gibbet at this spot in 1789 for murdering his young wife.

'A terrible story, Cottle. Poor fellow fell in love with Ann Rice, a local girl. But he was forced to marry another half-witted woman he didn't love.

Charcoal burners' fires

He couldn't bear the misery of it and murdered her.'

Cottle watches Coleridge shudder and turn pale. 'Wordsworth's writing a poem about it.' Coleridge stumbles on up the lane under the shadow of the old oaks, clearly upset. Then he turns: 'Poole was here, you know. He was part of the crowd watching the execution.'

*Whortleberries*

They turn off into thick woods. Coleridge, recovered, stamps off through the bracken to talk to some woodmen coppicing the young trees. Others are barking oaks for Poole's tannery. The ground all around is carpeted with whortleberries, still hard and not yet the dusty blue that shows they're ripe for picking. 'They're tasty, Cottle. I'll come here with Sara and Hartley at the end of July. And Poole and the Cruikshanks. We'll fill a basket or two and make a party of it. Sara will bake a delicious whortleberry pie.'

Finally the two young men emerge into the breezy open spaces of the Quantock Hills and Cottle gasps at the sudden panorama of the Welsh coast laid out below. Sailing ships are beating up and down the Bristol Channel. He hears Coleridge quoting: 'Some fair bark, perhaps, whose Sails light up / The slip of smooth clear blue betwixt two Isles / Of purple shadow'. He recognises the lines – they're from *This Lime Tree Bower My Prison*. Coleridge, as he had imagined his friend Charles Lamb would be in the poem, is standing overlooking the scene 'struck with deep joy', and 'silent with swimming sense'.

As they work their way down the slope Coleridge points to a lone thorn tree, gnarled and moss-covered. 'Wordsworth's written a poem about a Quantock thorn. A poor mad village woman buries her baby there'. Cottle shivers and looks away at the flowering gorse. Though majestic and beautiful, these lovely hills seem stricken with sadness and tragedy. 'Is that a fit subject for poetry, Sam?' 'Why not? Shepherds, beggars, drovers, idiots, they've all got stories that deserve telling.'

They head down Woodlands Hill to Alfoxden. Cottle hopes the meal will be better than the last one he had there. The 'stout piece of cheese' he had been looking forward to had been stolen and eaten by a rat. They'd dined on dry bread.

*The view from Woodlands Hill towards the Bristol Channel and the Welsh coast*

# BIRTHPLACE OF THE NEW POETRY

In July 1797 Coleridge was delighted when William and Dorothy Wordsworth found a suitable house to live in close to Stowey. Tom Poole had managed to negotiate a year's lease for the brother and sister on a substantial country house at Alfoxton, just beyond the village of Holford, five miles away. Coleridge's daily routine altered dramatically. He was just as besotted with the Wordsworths as they were with him. He walked over to Alfoxton almost daily, his path signposted today as the Coleridge Way.

*William Wordsworth*

was very different. The lanes and field paths would have bustled with people on the move. Most people worked within a mile of their homes, and country life was a noisy, public affair. Wagons rattled between villages; ploughmen stumbled through the furrows behind oxen teams; eagle-eyed shepherds watched from Will's Neck or Longstone Hill; and out in the wooded combes around Holford men were felling timber or barking oaks for Tom Poole's tannery.

### Strange behaviour
The paths and tracks were not used for recreation; they were a means of getting to and from work. If you were a gentleman, you made a point of not walking anywhere – if you were seen rambling in the country, your status was immediately in question. Where was your horse or chaise? Were you a vagrant or a thief? A murderer, even?

*Alfoxton, Holford*

**Quantock countryside now and then**
Stowey countryside today: silent lanes with only the occasional growl of a passing car; rooks squabbling overhead; the occasional surprised cat. Out beyond the farms, high up on the Quantock Hills, only ramblers, or a string of mountain bikers slithering along the muddy tracks.

The Stowey countryside that Coleridge and the Wordsworths knew two hundred years ago

*Holford Glen: 'The roaring dell, o'erwooded, narrow, deep …' ('This Lime Tree Bower')*

Characteristically, Coleridge and the Wordsworths ignored the rules of polite society and walked everywhere. Their unusual behaviour was a source of intense interest to the Quantock country people. They were especially curious about Wordsworth, who was seen to 'wander about by night, and look rather strangely at the moon'. And what was his real relationship with the gypsy-like young woman he lived with and whom he said was his sister?

## In pursuit of the sublime

The trio were deeply inspired by the teachings of the French philosopher Rousseau. Night and day they rambled the wild and rugged country of the Quantock Hills, abandoning themselves to the pursuit of the 'Sublime'. Squatting on camp stools, they drank in the dramatic prospect of the sea from Higher Hare Knap 'until it melted into more than natural loveliness'. They explored the romantic hidden dell at Holford Glen with its foaming waterfall. Coleridge and Dorothy basked in the moonlight on Stowey's castle mound, lying together on the grass in the darkness and silence. They jotted down their spontaneous responses in their notebooks – Dorothy had a fine eye for natural detail, and both poets, especially Wordsworth, relied on her record of their everyday walks when they composed their poems. Small and dark-skinned, she was fashionably prey to her emotions, laughing out loud, darting up and down the steep hills like a wild child of Nature, and letting her feelings run free. Coleridge adored her, and she him.

## Differing responses to nature

The two poets had differing responses to the Quantock countryside. Wordworth drew on close, direct observation of nature for his poems, and often wrote pacing methodically up and down the gravel path at Alfoxton. Coleridge's mind, on the other hand, was like a butterfly; the associations he made between the

## A word in edgeways

'He is very great in monologue, but he has no idea of dialogue.' MADAME DE STAËL

The poet Samuel Rogers confirms that Coleridge was 'a marvellous talker'. However, he recalls a meeting with Wordsworth during which Coleridge 'talked uninterruptedly for about two hours …' When they left, Rogers admitted to Wordsworth 'Well, for my own part, I could not make head or tail of Coleridge's oration: pray, did you understand it?' 'Not one syllable of it,' was Wordsworth's reply.

*First edition of 'Lyrical Ballads' 1798*

## Two extraordinary poems

Coleridge had the infuriating habit of wandering off on his own, often without giving Sara any idea of when he might return. In November 1797 he headed for Lynton, staying the night in a 'lonely farmhouse' near Culbone. Here he wrote his visionary poem *Kubla Khan*. His poetic inspiration was aided by 'two grains of Opium, taken to check a dysentery', and his account of the interruption by the 'person from Porlock' is one of the most famous stories in English literature. Whether true or not, the poetic fragment we are left with is enough to guarantee Coleridge's place amongst England's greatest poets.

natural world around him and abstract ideas were loose and intellectual. He composed while he walked. He had an 'almost visionary fondness' for the Quantock countryside. His observations and feelings were transmuted through the 'shaping power' of his imagination, which itself was moulded by his extensive reading – at this time he was fascinated by Gothic fantasy and exotic travellers' tales.

## 'Lyrical Ballads'

The two poets collaborated in the production of *Lyrical Ballads*, the ground-breaking anthology that ushered in the Romantic era of English poetry. Coleridge agreed to write pieces that were 'supernatural, or at least romantic', and Wordsworth to write about 'incidents and situations from common life' and 'the passions of men … incorporated with the beautiful and permanent forms of nature'. Most important of all, both poets were to write in the vernacular language and voices they heard around them in the Quantocks, as opposed to the formal, classical style of the 18th century.

*The Rime of the Ancient Mariner* had very different origins. The two poets were on a walking excursion, and planning to jointly write a ballad. It was to be based on the committing of a crime and Wordsworth suggested the shooting of an albatross. In the event, Coleridge wrote the entire poem himself. It was a long and complex work, and he returned to it time and again down the years, revising and rewriting. It remains his enduring masterpiece.

*Doré illustration (1876) for 'The Rime of the Ancient Mariner'*

# *imagine* ...
## Sara's day in the Lime Street cottage

❧ The mice play the very devil with us. It irks me to set a trap. By all the whiskers of all the pussies that have mewed plaintively, or amorously, since the days of Whittington, it is not fair. 'Tis telling a lie. 'Tis as if you said, 'Here is a bit of toasted cheese; come little mice! I invite you!' when, oh, foul breach of the rites of hospitality! I mean to assasssinate my too credulous guests! No, I cannot set a trap. ❧

S T COLERIDGE TO JOSEPH COTTLE, APRIL 1797

Collecting wood. Lighting a fire. The constant struggle to stop it smoking. Coleridge, head down in a book, hands flapping to keep the smoke from Hartley's eyes, telling Sara 'Sally Pally, isn't this simply paradise!'

A mouse scratches at the wainscot. Nappies steam on every chair back. She must remember to patch Sam's shirt. Oh, and the Wordsworths are coming this evening, so there's a pie to make and a ham to take to the baker's oven.

Sara sighs, then smiles, always ready to humour the husband she adores. A minute later, while changing Hartley in the dark back kitchen she hears a thud.

*The Kitchen*

Back in the parlour a pile of ironing has dropped into the dust and ash of the floor. Her husband has gone. He must have dislodged the ironing from the back of the chair when he jumped up.

Where's Coleridge? He's half way through the orchard on his way to Tom Poole's, ever keen to get away from the chaos:

'My dear Poole, I had to get away from the smoke. I can't write, I can't think with the infernal smoke. Ah, you've new books? Yes, I'd love a cup of tea.'

Sara's role: to make do. To make her husband and baby comfortable. To eke out their last bit of money.

# SARA COLERIDGE'S HARD JOURNEY

Sara Fricker has received harsh treatment down the years from critics. She was not the ideal wife for Coleridge, but it is equally true that he was not the ideal husband for her. The way her life and prospects turned out during the three years in Stowey must have been a terrible shock and disappointment to her.

## From respectability to bankruptcy

Sara was no stranger to tragedy. One of six children – she had five sisters – her childhood had been spent in and around Bristol in comparative comfort. At one stage the Fricker family had a country villa at Westbury, and enjoyed visits to fashionable Bath where they had a circle of smart friends. Everything changed in 1786 when she was just sixteen – her father went bankrupt and died soon after, a broken man. Suddenly bailiffs were banging on the door, carrying out the furniture and seizing the house. Mrs Fricker now found herself facing penury with six children to look after. Family life was turned upside down, and Sara and her sisters Mary and Edith were sent out to work as needlewomen to help keep body and soul together.

## A fatal attraction

In spite of this terrible setback Sara determinedly hung on to her pride and self-worth. She was witty and accomplished, read poetry sensitively, and was considered beautiful. Despite her poverty, she always made the best of herself, using her skills in needlework to create stylish gowns and dresses.

Coleridge's courting of Sara was an on-off affair. He was certainly attracted

*Sara Coleridge, when she was thirty-nine*

to her. His close friend the poet Robert Southey married Sara's sister Edith, and Coleridge eventually agreed to marry Sara. At first he was reluctant, then changed his mind, and finally fell head over heels in love. 'I love and I am beloved, and I am happy!'

## A sad fiddle-faddler?

Sara was intelligent and well-read, and could hold her own in most social gatherings. However, she was never going to be admitted to the 'sacred and privileged pale' of the Wordsworth literary circle, although Charles Lamb and John Thelwall were both very fond of her and sang her praises.

Dorothy Wordsworth, on the contrary, found Sara to be 'deficient in organic sensibility'. She even branded her a 'sad fiddle-faddler' as a housekeeper. This was almost certainly a grossly unfair accusation, as Sara's role as Coleridge's wife demanded that she be level-headed and practical. Coleridge was always full of promises and good intentions, but it was up to Sara to ensure that there was food on the table, not only for the family but for the many guests who arrived at Gilbards expecting board and lodging. Unlike Dorothy, Sara rarely had the opportunity to free her emotions in the fashionable 'Romantic' manner, to wander the Quantocks, or to indulge in literary debates late into the night. There was always a fire to light or a shirt to iron and, of course, there was baby Hartley to look after. And, to cap it all, she had a husband who was already showing the disturbing signs of addiction to laudanum.

So often she must have wondered: why isn't Sam writing? Why isn't he out on his vegetable patch as he promised? Where's the money draft from Cottle to pay the Stowey butcher? It's hardly surprising that she was often frustrated and a shade terse in manner, especially when she saw the husband she adored

*The restored well*

failing to give time and commitment to what Tom Poole called 'the common concerns of life'. She must have felt that she had exchanged a life of poverty with her sisters in Bristol for a life of drudgery and penury with her new husband – however much of a genius he was.

### Domestic tasks

Washing day was a particularly gruelling chore. Sara and Nanny would have to carry endless buckets of water from the well in the garden, turning the heavy windlass to raise the bucket. Then the water would have to be heated in a cauldron over the fire, before they pounded the clothes clean by hand.

Constant trips to the wood pile were necessary, and when money was particularly tight one of the family would go out into the surrounding countryside to collect wood. The maid, Nanny, showed a little too much initiative one morning. Coleridge, happening to rise at an earlier hour than usual, tells how he *'observed her putting an extravagant quantity of paper into the grate in order to light the fire, and mildly checked her for her wastefulness.'* Nanny replied *'La, Sir! Why, it is only Watchmen.'*

Such was the fate of the unsold copies of

*Unsold copies of 'The Watchman' with which Nanny lit the fire*

this short-lived periodical, the poet's first serious attempt at making money out of writing and publishing.

## A lonely and worrying time

Could Sara cook? It seems more than likely that she could. When she lived with her mother and sisters in Bristol they would surely have shared the household duties. Yet Coleridge, in a letter to Poole a month before he arrived in Stowey, said 'I will instruct the maid in cooking'. Coleridge himself complained later in 1803 about the 'Trash & general irregularity of Diet' at Stowey. Yet how much of this could be put down to the poor facilities at Gilbards, including the lack of a proper oven and the constant worries about money?

It must have been very lonely for Sara at times. The maid Nanny must have been a vital support and friend to her during the long and difficult periods when her husband was away. Nanny was very fond of little Hartley, and in later times would tell people how sorry she felt for Sara having to bear the brunt of life at Gilbards, and to bring up her child largely on her own.

# Stowey social life

Life at Stowey may have been hard for Sara but it was not all drudgery. When the Coleridges first arrived in Stowey they were viewed with suspicion because of the poet's reputation for being a radical. But their regular church-going and Coleridge's visits to Taunton and Bridgwater to preach in the Unitarian chapels slowly but surely allowed them to enter into Stowey's social life.

Sara became firm friends with Anna Cruikshank of Castle Hill House, who also had a baby of Hartley's age, Anna Elizabeth. She took tea with the Pooles, and was particularly friendly with Tom's old mother. Together with their influential guests the Coleridges would gather in Tom Poole's rustic arbour, enjoying tea under the spreading branches of the famous lime tree.

The Coleridges went to parties and dances and musical evenings. There were regular social gatherings in the Assembly Rooms at the Rose and Crown. They would have eagerly looked forward to these, joining in with the dancing and games of whist. Sara would keep a wary eye on her husband, as he enjoyed chatting to the young ladies of the village. Witty, and ever ready with a quip and a flattering comment, he would have quickly gathered an admiring coterie around him, giggling at his antics.

Coleridge would probably have been a member of the Stowey Book Society. Meetings were held at the Globe. The Over Stowey rector William Holland was a regular, as was Tom Poole. Members would spend an agreeable evening enjoying a good dinner and buying, selling and swapping books. You would be unfortunate if you bought a book from Coleridge, as it would doubtless have been smothered with his scribbled annotations.

# *imagine* ...
## the garden and Poole's lime tree bower

❝ Charles Lamb has been with me for a week – he left me Friday morning. – The second day after Wordsworth came to me, dear Sara accidently emptied a skillet of boiling milk on my foot, which confined me during the whole time of C. Lamb's stay & still prevents me from all walks longer than a furlong. – While Wordsworth, his Sister, & C. Lamb were out one evening; sitting in the arbour of T. Poole's garden, which communicates with mine, I wrote these lines, with which I am pleased … ❞

S T COLERIDGE TO ROBERT SOUTHEY, JULY 1797

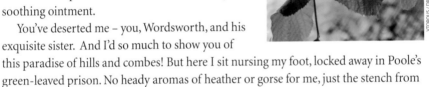

*July 1797.* So, dear Charles, you have visited us at last! You've exchanged your daily round of clerking and the crowded, noisy halls of East India House for the airy spaces of our beloved Quantock Hills, and the bright singing of larks.

But when you do finally come, what happens? Darling Sara, lovable but clumsy as ever – I know you dote on each other! – empties boiling milk over my foot. I howled louder than the banshees and had to hop down the street to Lewis for a jar of soothing ointment.

You've deserted me – you, Wordsworth, and his exquisite sister. And I'd so much to show you of this paradise of hills and combes! But here I sit nursing my foot, locked away in Poole's green-leaved prison. No heady aromas of heather or gorse for me, just the stench from his tannery.

Are you relishing the change of air, my friend? I'm wondering where you are. Did you stop for a glass at the Castle of Comfort among the copper miners? Are you now at Holford, marvelling at the roaring dell, peering over the dripping edge at the dark waters tumbling into the chasm below? A sublime place, indeed, and a worthy subject for verse! Maybe you're climbing out of Hodder's Combe up the steep path under towering beeches to the heights of Longstone Hill. How different to the smoke and din of dreary Leadenhall Street!

There was, as you will guess, a reason for my insistence on your visit. I wanted you for a blessed moment or two to forget the tragedy of last year. How is your sister Mary? But then how could anyone possibly forget the stabbing to death of their mother by their sister? Gentle-hearted Charles, my oldest friend since our days at Christ's Hospital, I know the burden you must carry through your life – your pledge to watch over your poor sick sister and to protect her from herself. My heart goes out to you.

A bat has just wheeled past. Rooks are streaming by bound for their roost, their black wings scoring the dusky air. Though I can't be with you to share your joy, there's life and beauty enough here for me. I now see that we must all keep our hearts and minds awake to love and beauty, no matter where we find it!

33

# This Lime-tree Bower my Prison

*Addressed to Charles Lamb, of the India House, London*

Well, they are gone, and here must I remain,
This lime-tree bower my prison! I have lost
Beauties and feelings, such as would have been
Most sweet to my remembrance even when age
Had dimm'd mine eyes to blindness! They, meanwhile,
Friends, whom I never more may meet again,
On springy heath, along the hill-top edge,
Wander in gladness, and wind down, perchance,
To that still roaring dell, of which I told;
The roaring dell, o'erwooded, narrow, deep,
And only speckled by the mid-day sun;
Where its slim trunk the ash from rock to rock
Flings arching like a bridge;—that branchless ash,
Unsunn'd and damp, whose few poor yellow leaves
Ne'er tremble in the gale, yet tremble still,
Fann'd by the water-fall! and there my friends
Behold the dark green file of long lank weeds,
That all at once (a most fantastic sight!)
Still nod and drip beneath the dripping edge
Of the blue clay-stone.
                          Now, my friends emerge
Beneath the wide wide Heaven—and view again
The many-steepled tract magnificent
Of hilly fields and meadows, and the sea,
With some fair bark, perhaps, whose sails light up
The slip of smooth clear blue betwixt two Isles
Of purple shadow! Yes! they wander on
In gladness all; but thou, methinks, most glad,
My gentle-hearted Charles! for thou hast pined
And hunger'd after Nature, many a year,
In the great City pent, winning thy way
With sad yet patient soul, through evil and pain
And strange calamity! Ah! slowly sink
Behind the western ridge, thou glorious Sun!
Shine in the slant beams of the sinking orb,
Ye purple heath-flowers! richlier burn, ye clouds!
Live in the yellow light, ye distant groves!
And kindle, thou blue Ocean! So my friend

Struck with deep joy may stand, as I have stood,
Silent with swimming sense; yea, gazing round
On the wide landscape, gaze till all doth seem
Less gross than bodily; and of such hues
As veil the Almighty Spirit, when yet he makes
Spirits perceive his presence.
                                        A delight
Comes sudden on my heart, and I am glad
As I myself were there! Nor in this bower,
This little lime-tree bower, have I not mark'd
Much that has sooth'd me. Pale beneath the blaze
Hung the transparent foliage; and I watch'd
Some broad and sunny leaf, and lov'd to see
The shadow of the leaf and stem above
Dappling its sunshine! And that walnut-tree
Was richly ting'd, and a deep radiance lay
Full on the ancient ivy, which usurps
Those fronting elms, and now, with blackest mass
Makes their dark branches gleam a lighter hue
Through the late twilight: and though now the bat
Wheels silent by, and not a swallow twitters,
Yet still the solitary humble-bee
Sings in the bean-flower! Henceforth I shall know
That Nature ne'er deserts the wise and pure;
No plot so narrow, be but Nature there,
No waste so vacant, but may well employ
Each faculty of sense, and keep the heart
Awake to Love and Beauty! and sometimes
'Tis well to be bereft of promis'd good,
That we may lift the soul, and contemplate
With lively joy the joys we cannot share.
My gentle-hearted Charles! when the last rook
Beat its straight path along the dusky air
Homewards, I blest it! deeming its black wing
(Now a dim speck, now vanishing in light)
Had cross'd the mighty Orb's dilated glory,
While thou stood'st gazing; or, when all was still,
Flew creeking o'er thy head, and had a charm
For thee, my gentle-hearted Charles, to whom
No sound is dissonant which tells of Life.

*1797*

# Coleridge's staunch friend, Tom Poole

*Tom Poole*

Tom Poole was born in 1766, the eldest son of a tanner. He was self-taught, his father refusing to allow him to go to university. His appetite for learning was voracious, and he amassed a library of books that impressed many eminent men of the day, including William Hazlitt and Charles Lamb. He was a committed radical, and sometimes offended the more conventional inhabitants of Stowey. However, his total lack of vanity endeared him to everyone.

From the moment the two men first met, Poole recognised greatness in Coleridge. Poole had the insight to see that he could be of immense help and support. In a letter of 1796 he wrote: 'By you, Coleridge, I will always stand, in sickness and health'. Coleridge escaped to the sanctuary of Poole's book room at the back of his house in Castle Street at every opportunity. It was in this room with its barrel roof that the Wordsworth and Coleridge circle met to talk and exchange ideas. (If you stay at Poole House, you can still see the book room today).

It is a measure of his quality that Poole enjoyed lifelong friendships with a number of influential men of the time, including Humphry Davy, the

*The outside steps to the bookroom*

Wedgwood brothers, and Andrew Crosse the scientist from nearby Broomfield.

Poole was a staunch and faithful friend to Coleridge to the end, even though they seldom met after 1807. He continued to offer financial support to Coleridge, advancing money for the periodical *The Friend*, and supporting Hartley at Oxford. He and Sara Coleridge shared a deep attachment, and they corresponded for many years after her separation from Coleridge.

*Scene in a tannery*

Tom Poole's legacy to Stowey is wide-ranging. As a landowner and owner of the family tannery, which he developed and expanded, he employed many local people. He was an active supporter of the Sunday School movement, formed the Stowey Female Friendly Society, and in 1812 donated the building for the village school (Stowey's library today). He died in 1837; you can see his grave and read his epitaph at the church.

# *imagine* ...
## Sara broods over her loss and sorrow

❝ Good night, my dear, dear Sara! – 'every night when I go to bed & every morning when I rise' I will think of you with a yearning love, & of my blessed Babies! – Once more, my dear Sara! good night. ❞

S T COLERIDGE TO SARA, FROM CUXHAVEN, GERMANY, SEPTEMBER 1798

*May 1799.* Sam, where are you? I need you. Why are you still in Germany? Which is more important, your family or your studies? It's eight months since you left us.

Samuel, our baby is dead. Berkeley, our beloved Berkeley! You've been told, so why aren't you here? We all thought he was getting better. He was over his bad reaction to the smallpox inoculation, but then he fell ill again. Lewis the apothecary said it was inflammation on his lungs.

Poole tells me you wrote to him saying you cannot truly say you are grieving for Berkeley. But that you are perplexed, and sad. Samuel, this is our son, our baby, who I sat through cold long nights with upon my lap, his poor little body burning like fire and scarlet all over. And just as he started to improve and I grew hopeful, he grew badly ill again. He died in my arms.

And no husband here to comfort me and share my grief. Oh Sam, you needed to have been here. You should have seen him – he was blind, poor little mite, his nose clogged, and so hoarse he couldn't cry. And he made the most horrible noise in his throat that terrified us all.

The good Poole has been here every day, and Catherine Cole – she suckled Berkeley for me when my breasts were swollen and painful. And all you could say in your letter to me in your good and honest Christian way was that you wouldn't give me words of consolation for fear it would fan into new activity the pang that you think is already growing dead and dull in my heart. Do you really think my pain is dulled? Sam, you don't know your wife any more. You've forgotten your home and you've forgotten all those of us who love you and depend on you.

I know you're studying German to justify the Wedgwoods' legacy and to safeguard our future. But you say it will take another six weeks and be June before you're back! And then to cap it all you wax on about shepherds and monks, how they ring bells in Germany, what the gallows are like there, drowned dogs and kittens … How can you expect me to take an interest in things like that now? Please, just come home. Your family needs you.

37

# A LONG, FATAL SEPARATION

*A scene in Germany, early 19th century*

The Quantock idyll began to unravel in May 1798, when the Wordsworths were told that their lease on Alfoxton was not to be renewed. Wordsworth was reluctant to search for alternative accommodation – he was never drawn to the Quantocks as strongly as Coleridge, and was already planning a return to his beloved Lake District where he was born and bred.

Coleridge knew in his heart that his prospects would not be advanced in remote, rural Stowey. He had a colossal thirst for knowledge, and now that he had the £150 annuity from the Wedgwoods he felt obliged to justify their faith in him by broadening his knowledge of philosophy, theology and other branches of learning. He suggested a tour to Germany with the Wordsworths. Sara was to go with them, but when a second baby, Berkeley, was born in May, it became impractical.

Coleridge and the Wordsworths sailed for Germany in September 1798. During the first weeks away he wrote long, touching letters to Sara, confessing to his homesickness. However, his enthusiasm for his new project soon took him over, and he enrolled as a student at the University of Göttingen, one of his aims being to write a book on the philosopher Lessing. He rambled over the surrounding hills, went to parties, and was soon enjoying himself. With his immense intellect and charm he soon amassed a circle of admiring friends:

*'Such an evening I never passed before – roaring, kissing, embracing, fighting, smashing bottles & glasses against the wall, singing – in short such a scene of uproar I never witnessed before ...'*

He also spent a sizeable sum of the Wedgwood money on books on metaphysics. Sara must have read his early letters with disbelief. Was he keeping a steady eye on his prospects? Did he have a firm grip on his family's financial security?

### A terrible tragedy

While Coleridge was away a number of Stowey babies were inoculated with smallpox vaccine. Berkeley reacted to it badly. As a result of the constant nursing and worry Sara herself fell ill: 'I was seized

*Innoculation against smallpox, by Louis-Léopold Boilly (1807)*

*A re-creation of an apothecary's workshop*

with a pain in my eye; it in a few hours became quite closed – my face and neck swollen, my head swimming …'

Berkeley recovered, but was ill again in November with a terrible cough. Lewis the Stowey doctor diagnosed it as 'inflammation on the infant's lungs'. Once again Sara spent interminable agonising nights nursing her baby. But Coleridge still did not come back. Deep in his studies, he wrote to Poole to say he would need three more months of work at Göttingen before he could return home. This news was a terrible blow for Sara. She had almost run out of money and had felt it necessary to move to Bristol where there was better medical help. Her hair had lost its lustrous colour and was falling out, and she cut much of

it off and took to wearing a wig. She was now desperate for her husband to come home. However Poole, believing that the study period in Germany was what was needed to safeguard the Coleridges' financial future, persuaded Sara to say nothing – bad news was certain to send his friend into a spiral of mental and physical decline.

Poor Berkeley died in February 1799. However, still Coleridge did not hurry home. He told Sara in a letter in early May that he was planning a walking tour through the Harz mountains, certain that his time in Germany would ensure their long-term prosperity. Finally he returned to England, arriving in late July after an absence of eleven months. Reluctant to face his wife, and unable to contemplate a return to life in Stowey, he stopped off in London, delaying his reunion with Sara still further.

Things were never to be the same again between the two. Sara was understandably hurt and bitter, and Coleridge was characteristically unable to confront his feelings of guilt and self-recrimination.

## Important German influences on Coleridge's thought

*Gotthold Lessing*
*Philosopher and*
*dramatist*
*1729-1781*

*Immanuel Kant*
*Philosopher*
*1724-1804*

*Friedrich Gottlieb*
*Klopstock*
*Poet*
*1724-1803*

*Friedrich Schiller*
*Philosopher and*
*dramatist*
*1759-1805*

# COLERIDGE'S LIFE AFTER STOWEY

The events in Coleridge's later life were increasigly shaped by his growing addiction to opium. He finally left Nether Stowey in September 1799, returning on just three occasions, in 1801-2, 1803 and 1807. Poole, as was to be expected, missed his friend badly, but remained loyal, and was always there with offers of help and support.

Coleridge worked as a successful journalist in London for the *Morning Post*, then moved with Sara to Greta Hall at Keswick in the Lake District. He was keen to save his marriage, but keener still to be near Grasmere, where the Wordsworths had moved. Wordsworth, however, had found his own unique poetic voice, and increasingly found Coleridge a disturbing influence, especially when he turned up unexpectedly, depressed and ill.

In 1804 Coleridge accepted the post of Secretary to the Governor of Malta. On his return to England two years later he moved back to the Lake District. Ill and troubled by the effects of opium, he finally separated from Sara in 1808, after a long infatuation with Sarah Hutchinson (Asra), a sister of Wordsworth's wife, Mary. For her he wrote the moving conversational poem *Dejection: An Ode*.

So began another phase in Coleridge's life. From this time onwards he lived in London, writing for the newspapers and lecturing, and compiling *Biographia Literaria*, his influential collection of thoughts on literature. He still wrote poetry – *Sybilline Leaves* was published in 1817 – but he never regained the magical touch of his Stowey days.

In 1816, his opium habit had grown so acute that he was accepted as a house patient by James Gillman, a London surgeon, who was partially successful in controlling his addiction. He lived with the Gillmans in Highgate until his death in 1834.

## Links

**The National Trust, Coleridge Cottage, Nether Stowey**
www.nationaltrust.org.uk/
coleridge-cottage

**The Friends of Coleridge**
www.friendsofcoleridge.com

**The Coleridge Way**
www.coleridgeway.co.uk

**General information about the Quantocks**
www.quantockonline.co.uk

**Bed and breakfast at Poole House**
www.poolehouse-quantocks.co.uk

## Further reading

**Coleridge and Wordsworth in Somerset**
Berta Lawrence, David & Charles 1970

**Coleridge: Early Visions**
Richard Holmes, Hodder 1989

**Coleridge and Wordsworth in the West Country**
Tom Mayberry, Alan Sutton 1992

**Samuel Taylor Coleridge: The West Country Years**
Reggie Watters, Friends of Coleridge 2011

**The Bondage of Love: A Life of Mrs Samuel Taylor Coleridge**
Molly Lefebure, Gollancz 1986

### Acknowledgements

Grateful thanks to Caroline Taylor (National Trust, Coleridge Cottage) and Tom Mayberry (Friends of Coleridge) for help and information.